Escape Velocity

Escape Velocity

Poems by

Kristin Kowalski Ferragut

Cover photograph by John Engle
Cover design by Shay Culligan

ISBN: 978-1-954353-29-9

Kelsay Books
502 South 1040 East, A-119
American Fork, Utah, 84003

Acknowledgments

Anti-Heroin Chic: "A Few of My Favorite Lost Things," "Second Chances," "Unbearable Lightness"

Beltway Poetry Quarterly: "Drowning," "Escape and Loss," "Eyes of the Dead," "Family Dinner: A Metaphysical Check-In," "Oracle of the First Kiss"

Bourgeon: "Transgendered Ex at Son's Birthday Party," "Vacuum"

Fledgling Rag: "A Twenty-Four-Year-Old Getting Two Dozen Roses at Forty-Nine: A Dialogue with Myself," "Life Care Planning"

Little Patuxent Review: "Underneath Quarantine"

Maryland Bards Poetry Review 2020: "Like It's New"

Mojave He[Art] Review: "The Enormity of It"

Nightingale & Sparrow: "Leaves of Late November"

Poems from the Lockdown: "When Screens Replace Touch"

The Magnolia Review: "Change Takes Energy," "Midlife Legacy," "Path of Lightning," "The One There Behind Me," "Whispers Enough" revised

The Novice Writer: "The Clotheshorse"

This Is What America Looks Like: Poetry and Fiction from DC, Maryland, and Virginia: "The County Fair"

I also thank the talented and cool group of local poets who've motivated and supported me in the past few years, especially those brave souls who share work and feedback in workshops. Lucinda Marshall, Alison Palmer, Serena Agusto-Cox, Indran Amirthanayagam, and Luther Jett have been particularly invaluable, generously providing insightful and ongoing reactions to my work. Finally, I thank my long-held Poet Friends, Don Soifer, Dizzy, Mabel Ferragut Smith, Kelly Catharine Bradley, and Tracey Lenhardt, who have seen many phases of me and my writing, and treated every one of them with patience and encouragement.

Thank you to all the wonderful literary journals that have published my poems and to Kelsay Books for publishing this collection and so many beautiful others.

Contents

III. At Rest

IV. In Motion

I. Reaction

You Say We're Like Magnets

Let's talk about magnets and electricity, how like poles
    repel,
how stirring is all that's needed
    to make energy.

Let's talk breath, blood, iron and the fever
    you got in the hotel
room when you allowed me to wipe your brow.
    Remember

you so still, my orbiting around you? how you wanted
    to stay.
Remember staying? The current versus
    the potential so rare in

your moving on. Let's talk about wind, water,
    heat and steam
that fuel movement to change charges to make objects
    attract.

Let's talk about the center of the earth, the magnetic field
    protecting
us from the sun, how you crushed the hornet's nest outside my
    window.

Let's talk about how you laugh when I say time
    is relative, then note
I'm right and laugh again, your eruption, my explosion. Let's
    talk about

quantum physics and how things take up more space
    when still than when
in motion. Let's talk about magnets not needing to touch
    to exert force.

Let's talk about your relationship to nickel, how your silver hair
    shines,
how I align more closely with copper, the common penny trying
    so hard.

Variation on Evolution

Salt bearing value of weight like diamonds, like
gold, currency in 2000 B.C., rain in the northern

Mojave Desert. Salt and spice, tremors of the best
kind, the making of continents, merging of mountains.

A little funny, gender wars and celebration of She.
Much to love in women, rich with nuance and passion,

moonlight and ocean, guardians of a species, but not
to the exclusion of He. Voicebox that undulates—

teasing target for kisses above naked flat chest sloping
to the root of countless jokes, infinite mysteries, always

decisive. I honor the definitive even when wrong, relief
to my spiraling, meandering, having no idea. I hear

sperm can now be made of bone marrow. I hear the Y-
chromosome lacks genetic diversity, hints toward

extinction. I'll take the pandemic, in-my-face
news, bombs, exploding need and guilt, God's game of

hide-and-seek. Grateful these are my times, with bearable
seasons and fruit bearing trees, while we still have men.

Waning When the Moon is Waxing

If only we fell like snowflakes, never
crashing, never boring, not loud.

We're only human, whirling
in our individual little confoundations.

We stuff a sock in it to muffle words, think
of something else, turn away. We're not

all good actors. Some of us have to
not care to look like we don't care.

I pray to the god of apathy every day.
Using our passions against each other,

we try to look sane with poor aim and lack
of wherewithal while we tamp down

things intended for keeps—singing,
chutzpah, ardor, the want to be heard

in the rare conversation that matters.
Just shovel it away, the sooted snow.

What the Alchemist Knows

Befriending the misanthropic with a wave of the hand;
evoking laughter through well-crafted phonemes;
disintegrating clothes to ash on the floor with breath.

Arms steady as though holding something precious;
perceiving sound versus noise with discerning ears;
waiting and forcing the wait.

Observing evidence of impact and studying
the transformation of unremarkable into beauty,
acknowledging everything but his own witchery.

Intermittentamorous

I turn off desktop, bedside lamp,
keyboard I force my son to practice.
But anything left plugged in bleeds energy.

Too much iron lost in blood causes
fatigue. Comes down to little mattering except
the one long hug, a lean in to be held up.

Memories feed the current. Hikes to sunsets,
after-parties, not-so-great-music sung boldly, the soup
so soothing I was almost glad for the mono.

Little else matters until it does. Time
for all else, focus on reliant others like chains, but more
like salvation, fights that can't be skirted.

Identifying as intermittentamorous is exhausting.
The on and off, yin/yang, dream
of love versus hope of freedom.

Feels like a long practice to learn to be done,
a sigh and unplugging. Skin intact, space for sleep
and a nod to the vast possibilities in silence.

Path of Lightning

What of lightning?
    the way water conducts electricity, the
        way we conduct ourselves
           in goodbyes, the jolt
        enough to stop a heartbeat;
           the second strike that can restart.
    Dispersed in water electricity travels
        only six meters, they say.

Drifting in her upthrust beside
    my sea, a thousand
        kilometers south.
You reaching
    past having failed
        to lay down short term memory. I
        having failed
to be memorable.
Young love incites, even at a distance,
        even when old.
           You reach for her.

But what of fish and birds?
    Migrating trout eating fried crayfish; scooped
        by swoops of ospreys,
           dropped in path of a hungry bass,
           traveling to near you.
Not much for swimming, but you do love
    bare feet. You feel
        the current. So you don't
           sleep with her.

Never mind that it's July.
We're all mystified—ospreys and gulls, bass and trout,
        you and I.

        Me, treading water, never one for touching
                the ocean floor; you walking
        away, me confusing seaspray with
                        rains; you wildly shooing
                sandflies, looking like a dance.
The only element that matches
                the season is the wishing.

What Escapes Our Lips

Shifty sharp truth hides
in the hippocampus, sometimes
trashing the place.

Lost in both guilt
and good intentions, the most fragile
of virtues parcels reason to skirt itself
sure as a blackjack dealer hitting
a kid who holds ten. It sneaks in behind
molars; escapes in bits through
spittle and carbon dioxide,
despite the best effort of lips.
Once out, it grows like expandable water toys
from the dollar store. It strobes
like a murder of grackles beating wings
between ground and midday sun. It stifles and
strangles in sweet, like the scent
of the lilac tree from childhood.
Makes us cough.

Truth visits at night, disrobes,
measures shape of hips, size of freckles,
shades of moles.
Contrasts might keep us up all night.
Tired at daybreak, soft things grow
—mauve sunrise, chenille comforter, silence.
Truth leaves words in shambles.

Bodyguard

I draw a sunburn
with midday July over
cheeks, shoulders, hidden
thighs. From monochromatic
to shades of ways we take
coffee and Red Dye 40
mixed with sweet. If I absorb enough
heat, blood might simmer
through winter. If scorched I'll shirk
from touch, a welcome cooling.

Summer of You

Everywhere I travel, tall stalks
of orange waterfalls have me
think this The Summer of
Tiger Lilies. Bold and contrary
the way they stand tall
just to bow down over clover
like the way you love while
bowing out, always.

They move to a chorus
of cicadas and
bees veering in breezes like how
you dance, knees crossing,
curving, back rounding,
like wind-smoothed edges.

Hard to pass a cluster without
hearing the Peter Pan song.
Thoughts turn to you who won't
wear suits and how I tried to rescue
you from words like swords.
I am no Tiger Lily.

On the wall in my rented room,
a painting of Tiger Lilies, one
blossom fallen and curled, beside
my bed. Been years since
we split, but sometimes beds
still remind me of you.

A Twenty-Four-Year-Old Getting Two Dozen
Roses at Forty-Nine: A Dialogue with Myself

24.

I want no part of
the kill. Stems cut above the
roots for a gesture.

49.

Dried flowers scattered
about in vases remind
me of fresh smiles.

24.

No clichés in snap
dragons or cacti, but those
conceited roses!

49.

Grateful for symbols—
a cross, a peace sign, a rose,
things that cut through fog.

24.

Roses' watery
scent calls to mind mother's soap,
less than alluring.

49.

I lean close to catch
the fragrance. Petals tickle
my lip like a kiss.

24.

Hard to believe. I
try to, despite myself, while
saying, "Love is death."

49.

Tearful with age, but
emboldened I embrace Faith,
strong enough for risk.

Mr. and Mrs. Bomaye Meet Well-Timed End

We watched *Ali* on
thirteen inch screen from
hand-me-down
futon, the only
incarnation of life
that hosted a tv in my
bedroom. Hard to see
up on dresser, audio
was everything: your
hand stirring popcorn,
dialogue, your breath,
"Ali Bomaye!" On brink
of till death do us part
we fell in love with the
chant. Henceforth we called
us Mr. & Mrs. Bomaye.
Later I learned it meant
"Kill him." Much later
you left; the same year
Mohammad Ali died.

Family Dinner: A Metaphysical Check-In

Angst of youth, elemental.
Global warming, yes,
but we shrunk the hole in
the ozone; the Gulf War
did not annihilate us;
Malthus was proven wrong.
Humans are smart, despite
evidence to the contrary.
An obligatory dinner
turned essential discussion.

Bullies tend toward half-wit
"You're ugly and stupid,"
as though creativity isn't
gorgeous. So we discuss
ingenuity and comebacks,
places for help, space
for ignoring, and expansive
possibilities in the transcendental,
or even God.
No one wants the night to end.

Full of doubt too, I check
myself against pop psychology—
parents it seems cause all Gen Z's
anxiety. *Do I solve*
too many of your problems?
Do I pressure you to be happy?
No, they console, as miserable
as I was in '87, fretting the
the end of the world.

Change Takes Energy

Thunderstorms rotate into hurricanes, rockets hit
escape velocity over 25 thousand miles per hour, birthday cake
bakes at 350 degrees to tender perfection. No reason to expect

any leftovers. Babies can't loan you thirty bucks
and butterflies won't take out the trash upon emerging
from the chrysalis. And she isn't the one with whom

you tied the knot, fumbling hands recalling torn-through
mittens on the rope tow because the hill was just too
steep and you never did learn to ski. Gloriously

happy with the band on your finger, all that hide and seek
behind you. He wouldn't keep you safe or bring you
soup, but still a kind of resting place. Buried beneath

pills and knives, scars and scarves, you'll never find
him now. You fueled the escape and don't quite begrudge
it, except in what is misunderstood as finite. All these

worries of loss overlook what science shows us—renewable
energy in wind, tides, sun, your heart and the smile
you give your kids after taking out the trash.

Like It's New

The lonesome in being young sharpens.
Coming of age in the 80s, the older
look at lips of those younger like murder.
Parents won't share a sip, even if it's alcohol.

One hundred thousand dead and dying.
An epidemic feels just like a pandemic if
you're in the wrong place at the wrong time.
Two AM at Boothill Saloon Cemetery can't be

the right place except when I knew
he shot crack through his veins and I might stop him.
I suppose we all want to die a bit anyway, especially
me when he eluded being found. Invisible like viruses.

Still we hunt in sideways looks at others, supposing
the cleanliness of fingernails or shape of eyes might
expose harbored sickness. Harbor grudges

for the skateboard thrashers, always at the parks sharing
hi-fives and Pepsis. Selfish youth in congregation
of laughter and risk, intent on killing us all. As though
it's not the time of their lives.

Neat with pockets to hold cell phones not fistfuls
of quarters, husbands, second husbands, cats, dogs, debt,
music and the ceaseless bad news. We hide in our homes
and act as though we've never seen a plague before.

II. Force

Repress Nothing

I don't care
if you throw the tire iron
to clank against pavement, as
long as you miss my bones.
"What I miss?" you
may ask the morning
after. If you howl and never
explain, it's because you
never need a reason.

I don't care
if you come late and
stay too long, even if
you don't say a word.
You can even leave early,
though I'd miss
the sigh, weep, crow
of your breath. Most
importantly, repress nothing.

I don't care
if you cry like a toddler
missing his plushy, or
suck your thumb if you
have to; hell, you can even
suck mine. Whatever it
takes keep it circulating—
air, water, blood, ardor—
it all needs cleansing.

When You Close the Door

We trade Irish Step, German folk claps and stomps for
sways and circles. Everything turns Latin when

the moon issues dares, candles light and you close
the door. We spill upon covers, agave syrup, cinnamon,

salt water. Space turns outside in, air in shared breath, long
refrains, shake of maracas and rain sticks beneath roof under

stars we wish on even when blanched by midday summer sun.
We follow tails of meteors, draw constellations in freckles,

moles, scars. Every song that plays—the best song ever. Time
of lucid dreams or subconscious wakefulness in skin and motion.

We never dance the Salsa or Tango at the bar, but later play
wandering minstrels, drum rhythms on each other's hips.

The Enormity of It*

Look to desert, rock, gila monster, the ease
of one thin layer on a hot day. Oh, but
the mirages! Maybe every beautiful boy just wants
to be a beautiful girl, protected, seduced;
to be swept...

off. Quivering words like blades of seagrass
whirl. Hard to know from where sounds come under
water. Ganymede raining down; always
the beautiful boys! Bound to Aquarius
though gazing far...

off. I pass along details of another Comcast
failure. Speak of missed meetups, late arrivals. Did
you hear? The things unsaid, the enormity of
it. Things not written or spoken, only perceived
in the trailing...

off. Gurgling, trickling, babbling flow of
missing and mercy can carve stone as well. But
to smash rocks to gravel in anger
is infinitely easier and better received.
Rain runs...

off. Have you tried singing under water? It's most
fun alone, even if you dislike the company.
Self-hate and hating life are two distinct
states, but neither worth fretting. If hate fails
to kill, it burns...

off. Burdens lie in the apple seed your mother
warned would grow to a tree in your belly.
Grief, love, grace—things that might fill a desert
sky at night; stay awake, look for Aquarius, as
Ganymede takes off.

*Title inspired by Kelly C. Bradley

Drowning

What was the cause of death?
What is the difference? When
life is terminal and living on
        so
                long.
Dirge is my dance.

You think *move on.*
I challenge you to
        Unzip your skin and see
        if you make it to the West Coast.
Exactly.

His life was not devastating to me.
Miracle of Lazarus echoed in
        one
                more
                        song
        again and again, 'till I almost
took them for granted.

He died of drink.

Deplorable, your eyes declare,
the debased death of
        a drunkard.
That's my devotion.

Dissonance in experience versus wanting
        to speak,
                to whom
                        for what.
Preferring the company of his grave or
        memory.

Quiet is not discordant and there is
        no silence;
not at the stone, with the breeze,
amidst tree frogs so
        fucking loud I can barely
hear his voice play back in mind.

Escape and Loss

Note: "Dziadeck" (dzadɛk) is Polish for grandfather

When fires catch and spread, flee
before the smoke drowns you.
What can't you leave without?
Your hat? The one your Dziadek gave
you when he moved to the old folks' home—
the place your Dad never visited.
The pictures of you with your first love?—
ones in which you barely recognize
wanton smile and clear eyes.
Your dog who's too old to jump or
fetch and will need to be carried outside
four times per day for the rest of her days?

What of when worry spreads, a
thick smog. Might stay with shallow
breaths for a bit, wave wildly to shoo thickness
away. But what do you grab if you run?
Do you gather his burdens? Hold them fast
in memory, refusing to fully unfurrow your brow,
as though it relaxes his?
Do you take trinkets that remind you of happy
days, the whole week's worth, to remember
as though they were the whole life?
Do you take the hat and pictures and dog, as though
birth certificate and wedding license mean nothing?

What do you leave?
Guilt hides beneath fingernails;.
sorrow clings to laughs' underbellies,
they will escape despite you.
But you might leave regret and waters

that douse the flames. If you have a choice,
you might leave anything that weeps.

Abandon things without breath,
lamps and games, and some things that breathe,
plushies who hold secrets, the melody
of "Why Me Lord?" rolled out in baritone waves.
Leave things too heavy to carry—hope chests,
jade plants, stooped shoulders—
things that shackle,
anything that prevents fast flight.

Transgendered Ex at Son's Birthday Party

I think to change into a t-shirt,
    something in which I can chase kids with water guns,
        something that disregards cleavage and shoulder.

You arrive in a pretty little dress.
    It's edgy, a sweetheart neckline
        white with black trim and little crickets and bees
        perched about.

And those legs, the sort I've always wanted—long and lean.
    Why do boys always have the best legs?
        No saddlebags or cellulite, but smooth
        exclamation points.

Your legs point up beyond the flared skirt to your new chest that
    I don't recognize.
I adjust my shirt, the one I will not change out of,
    the one that is not unisex.
        And I reapply my colored lip balm, the same
        as yours, I gave you last Winter.

I give you a hug and you feel dewy, like a woman glistening.
Never before good at forgetting, I cannot now remember
    what it was like to be yours.

I hesitate when introducing myself as his mom, with a glance
    towards you.
I see your mascara as a challenge and think that I should accent
    my eyes more.
        More feminine and brave, I see you as a Goddess,
        as supernatural as real.

I wish I kept that man I met after you left, the one
      with linear thoughts who told me women are from Venus
           and I talk too much. But only briefly
        just to have someone to steady me for a moment.

I avert my eyes as you bend to pick up a candle, a shock
      of electric blue peeking out.
I imagine the men I might meet—Tom with the spiky
      beard that might rub a rash on my face
        when we kiss. Glenn who rides a motorcycle.

You embrace your son and it looks like a parent holding
      birthday wishes close to the boy.
No change can render that image unforgettable and for a moment
      again I am yours.

Belonging

I'm little more than a tree—swing, home,
furniture, landscape, paper to draw away
nightmares. Not visitor, friend,
flock, company, novel, twinkling
lights, trouble-maker, twelve-year-old.
Not enough to cut the string
of his dull days.

Carried by a wave of teammates
from the game, roaring in a cloud
of cousins, sneaking out to meet
his pack at the clubhouse, building
bridges together. I dream for my boy.
He sleeps alone.

Lights on, ghouls peek from cracks
of louvered closet doors, giant
spiders nest outside his window.
The stuffed puppy stopped
whispering to him months ago.
Nothing means much without
one person to hold secrets.

Saints exist for beekeepers, lost
causes, gravediggers, lepers, travelers,
teachers, television, bacon.
No Patron Saint of belonging,
the one thing to comfort him,
to stave off lonely.

Unbearable Lightness

Anyone whose goal is 'something higher' must
expect someday to suffer vertigo.
—Milan Kundera, *The Unbearable Lightness of Being*

Tethered to nothing, we inhale deep enough to ache in hopes
that the weight of air will anchor us. When that fails, for ballast

we conjure memories of lost teddy bears, chipped teeth, the one
that got away, and what we wanted to be when we grow up.

We cling to the heft of agenda books and plans—fragility
that crumbles easily and drifts off as dust.

The list of things we believe hold us breaks our hearts when
they dissolve, like playing house.

There ought be a word for psychosomatic hope. The air
is full of things blown away from us—receipts of appliances we

wanted to return, trash from the car floor, diplomas never
hung on walls, romance, hobbies we wanted to be our lives.

We anchor ourselves in burdens, lost causes, anything in shadows
of love, to keep from floating away, hearts and stomachs empty.

Vacuum

Not a heavy weight, more like
carrying around the five extra
pounds from the holidays all year.
Or maybe more like something one
picks up and sets down repeatedly,
like a little screaming baby, rattling
the nerves; one that is never
comforted and never grows up.
Or maybe slightly more weight that
one takes up every several days,
much like the weight of that heavy
vacuum you took from your
Mami's house. Too unwieldy for
me to use, I say, but you oppose
discarding it. The carpets fill with
fur and dust bunnies take permanent
residence in the corners and beneath
the keyboard no one ever plays.
Thinking to lighten the air, I buy my
own vacuum, bid adieu to those
cute, mini tumbleweeds and groom the
carpet. Still, this weight. It's most like
the way you look at me, wishing.

Distancing of Stars

It shows no sign of disappearing, the bite
just southeast of my hip bone, distance

from bay to open sea, from Betelgeuse to
Sirius, from open windows to dog days of

summer. Remember the afternoon? Deserted
strip of beach, not as in barren or empty, more

like the first morning stretch of body
enjoyed alone or beside one not seen as "other."

Spiders, snakes, midges—our congregation. What
did they see as we laid on sand in devotion

to sun, water, touch? Luncheon meats, invasive
species, fools in love? I didn't notice the mark until

nightfall, alone, then scratched through sleep. Weeks
later I try to predict when the shades grow deep

with ripened itch—with fatigue, storms, cut of my jeans?
The mark outlasts you. At high tide of your disinterest

it burns in shades of purple. I wear your mood
ring on thigh, this body I have less use for.

Moonlight's Secrets

Folks think they fear
dark but it's really
the night; no, it's whispers
of the moon
raucous in their hypnagogic
state. She murmurs
into space where they pine and
mourn. She speaks in ripples
and surges, tugging at
waters of hearts and thighs; promises
solace and illumination.
They find belief
more frightening than
the lonesome. Relieved
when too full the Moon spills,
her secrets, casting
"I lie" with light on the creek.

Oracle of the First Kiss

Go, return not die in war.
    —Oracle of Delphi

The primeval conversation, perceived
in spirographic circles about the flesh and
breath and air above inscribes. Hints of

meaning, more about the shape of what's
missing, or about flight than weight.

Reclined and entwined, inhalation harmonizing
over everything—fingerprints, limbs,
eyes reluctant to open…Everything.

In the rustle and wrestling, the Oracle speaks.
"Continue not drown in lonesome."

No matter. A moment widens, wills
eternity to unfold. One tear, no more, shed
for those forsaken.

Silence, but for vowels drafted in air with hips and
the Oracle's whisper. Divine fortune in tracks

of the taste of iron traced by the tongue in places
lips have worn thin. Read rug burns from
stubble like tea leaves, concluding "Love will prevail."

Consider that, while trying not to spill in zero-gravity. With
knots worked out of muscles, what's to hold together?

Whispers Enough

She wanted to love like
    a whisper;
        Him leaning
in, breath on
    cheek; listening.
        Her lips curved
upward reaching for
    sky; his hands holding
        hips to anchor
them both, a kind of home.

Nests, cabins, caves—
    homes as well. She considers
        tapestry or making do.
He speaks of "push me pull you"
    wondering if tides
        can cut
ties to the moon;
    as though she could shut up,
        as though he'd be still.

He thinks it better to savor
    the puddle than pine
        for the ocean.
She figures it matters little if
    they're both mirages.
        They rock
into the night waiting on
    the day there's a day after
        the hangover.
Some mornings they both whisper.

Second Chances

I want to knit swatches of
Egyptian cotton, wrap your
scars in shades of sky; fill the
furrow of your brow with sheer
layers of gloss from kisses.
      Over years.
Peace made through surrender, still
loss. Holes may close as well as
fill. Then what space is left?
      Things unloosed:
dulcet rifts or discordant
riffs, bedrock.
If salt water cured ailments
of memory I would weep
over cup, offer it as
though from Lourdes with prayers for
comfort. This is what they mean
      by second chances;
To put the blood back
      in the stone.

Midlife Legacy

It's not so much that I love my Vintage
'69 tee, my "maybe it'll help me get used
to being 50" winter tax refund splurge when
spring hovered at a civilized distance.

I wear it a lot but imagine it a less deliberate
buy; two bucks at a thrift store and worn
thin, a comfortable absence of shape, maybe
bought by someone else. Twenty years hence

a twenty-something girl sifts
through racks, discovers a grey, v-neck
"Vintage '69" tee. Wears it to an Imagine
Dragons reunion concert where the band wears

baseball caps and shouts lines a little hoarse.
She's unsure of the guy she's with until they stop
at the peak of a bridge en route
to home and he wraps his arms around her hips.

She meets him like a sunburn.
Bats dart above. There might be other
people in the world, but she wouldn't know.
This guy is everyone and she suddenly loves

them all their fingertips and lips,
grasps and surprises. He wrinkles
her soft shirt in hand. Kisses deep enough
to catch her breath upon remembering at 50.

III. At Rest

If Eulogies Read Like IEPs

Individualized Education Programs (IEPs), required for each student receiving Special Education Services in the U.S., include objective measures of Present Levels of Performance and Goals. They are updated annually.

She demonstrated relative strength
in solving simple equations but required
support to solve multi-step word problems.

She appeared to like reading, exhibited
comprehension in discussions but scored
no more than 25% on multiple choice tests.

She presented as suspicious, each test item
a trick question. She applied creative thinking
to determine three out of four answers correct.

She showed ability to work efficiently but required
deadlines to submit assignments on time.
She performed inconsistently on most tasks.

Took on too much. Did too little.
Lacked perspective to know this millennium
is not a Renaissance. She required reminders

that dinnertime came every fucking night.
Although observers note she acted weird
she maintained efforts to seem normal, until

she didn't. Her relative strengths appeared
to be of disposition rather than effort. Realizing that,
she sustained high scores on being an enabler.

In some assessments, she had been labeled
a "misanthrope." It seems likely
that if she sought one out for dialogue ever

she appreciated that individual profoundly.
With her Social Emotional challenges in verbal
communication, that may have been unclear.

She smiled with communication partners 70%
of the time but benefited from less news and more
silence, to keep from crying nine out of ten days.

She achieved her long-term goals of not being locked up
nor killing anyone, but recent present levels indicate lack
of organization, memory skills, and reality-based thinking.

Although difficult to quantify, she self-reported strengths
of "good luck" and "authenticity." She rarely judged
others and although testing indicated significant weaknesses

she hoped her children would not blame her for inherited
or learned fears, neuroses or psychoses, unless it helped
them get through life. She exhibited contempt for Psychology.

Claiming a Moment

Sweet scents swing to clapping leaves and
crooning birds.
       Breeze on which there's floating.

Bees tease crape myrtle flowers, hover shy
of touch. A bluejay lands long enough
       for a prayer.

Mindfulness calls for appreciation and also
a taking for granted. To guard
moments against all they're not—enclosures,
shackles, EKGs, bare feet on ice.

Also present in burdens ignored is gratitude; also,
       "There but by God's Grace"; also,
       "What can be done?"

Two minds cut short in study
of myriad shades of green,
grow back as four minds cut short in shapes
of turns taken by sun and wind on limbs
       and grow again.
A Hydra unleashed; heads
oriented toward all compass tick marks
question whether the prayer is
of thanksgiving, intercession or repentance.

Not mutually exclusive. But even the Hydra
       has only one heart.

When Screens Replace Touch

Invisibility I say when my son asks
what superhero power I would choose.

I wasn't much older than he is when I set
my goal to be a disembodied spirit.

Think I'll have that one day because I'm lucky.
I'd forego touch if I could go unseen, but I'd rather

have it all—the feel of wind and fingertips,
skin and hair and be out of sight.

Fond of woods, yurts, and tents for their
simple beauty it's true, but also their lack

of mirrors. I don't perceive a movie of me when
we talk, which is why it scares me when you ask

*Why do you look like that? Why did you make
that face?* How do I know? I can't see me.

A man once responded only
to my words; he held still to my

hand through grimace, shrug, even tear never
asking. I tag him the one that got away.

Can't faces be just about the rest—breath,
blinks, kisses, sustenance, and not freckles and

wrinkles, pretty eyes and cute noses, crooked
teeth and dark circles.

Yet here we are. You watching me, and me watching
me and I don't know where else to look.

Nothing Hidden

Pictographs of laughter
on walls, heart and space
between words where he
rises. I think I prefer him
facing my gaze, surveying
precious things—forehead,
mouth, collar bones, thighs,
knees, until dimples on his
lower back almost wink.
I marvel as he walks away.

Stranger Things: Hopper's Demise

Feels good to cry over something
other than you. I let the tears,
don't wipe them away. Sucker
for a sad backstory and I waited

three seasons for him to kiss her,
but death. I hang this unrequited love
on nightmares and daydreams. Welcome
tween and teen who reach out and around
me, grasp hands, hug shoulders.

No time to take touch for granted. Who
will cry least? I rarely win. They feel bad
asking me to watch, although amused
that I weep. Funny really, a middle-aged

woman crying over a rebel sheriff in a fictional
town besieged by a Dungeons and Dragons
based-character. Funnier still the way
it makes me miss the scent of your cigarettes.

Hiding from the Ghost

Not our beer-soaked weekends, late-morning check-ins,
calls to end cap the day. End caps like Lowe's aisles of

electrical tape and weed killer or maybe more like sentimental
CDs displayed in a record store. Not wishes or plans.

But places void of you. Beside your transaction slips
I kept ledgers of time not filled by you—within

my height-of-summer confusion over sweat, dry, wet,
a/c chills; under mourning of other men; upon my skin

touched by a puff of breeze; submerged in a body of water.
I hide in rain, snow, heat, things you dislike, extremes, my

howling, fever, silence, exercise, whimsy. I move
a chunk of the soundtrack to storage. Few favorite haunts

let me give up the ghost of you, so I stay home. Console
myself that each friend will only ask about you one more time.

Life Care Planning

"Emergency Contact"
reads lonesome as
a blown tire on a solo
road trip or the rise
and fall of "feel like Sugar
on the Floor," crooned by
Etta James live.
But there's nothing so
romantic in a Kaiser
examination room.

Identify a Health
Care Agent, an alternate
and an alternate two,
directs the workbook.
"The doctor wants
you to fill this out."
Nurse hands it over like
a bouquet of hemlock.

Names flit
around the room,
not one wants
to sit on a line.

Sugarloaf Pet Gardens

He parks his car
beside the other one
in the gravel lot,
looks perplexed walking
between stones, stops,
takes off his hat
and bows his head.

He doesn't look up
immediately
with the gunshot,
hunting season
in far off woods.

Everything's done
in solemnity.
Later he looks
toward the source
of the resounding boom.
Now only an echo
in memory.

Solemn Playground

Death only writes the lines other thoughts lie
on in the cemetery where sacred ground gives

whiff of protection. Curved marble, slate, granite,
strong edges, matte or lustrous, cradle names

that string my steps together, a rosary walking
from stone to stone within quiet. I hold

them as evidence of mortality called to across
ten generations, as near forever as I can imagine.

Buried bone has mass, as do ashes of bone, vessels
of those that loved pets, worked fifty-hour weeks,

wrote, dreamt of heaven or hell or being reincarnated
as their favorite animals—rhino, lion, eagle, red panda.

Something more sounds in the "whoosh" of wind
that rustles leaves, musses up hair, cools my trickle

of sweat in the graveyard. Memories of tunes in the key
of my childhood incite—walking Kiki, sledding, forgetting

my parents' warning of Hell's Angels. I heard engines
but never saw a one. Stray mourners as still as stone carry

isolation in their grief. I'm as covert as the dead. They take
no notice of my bike washing past, guitar strummed

at a distance, protracted study of how green leeches to grey,
even my low laughter shared with the dead like a toast.

The Clotheshorse

It's in the clotheshorse—rock
behind which the goblin hides; profile
of the witch waiting to turn; shoes of the Giant.

Light from the street filters through stubborn
maples to backlight occupants—robbers, bats,
my mother's mourning, among others.

Unwise to close eyes amidst the dangers,
I study the shapes that tremble slightly through shadows
of wind-possessed leaves. In the betweens I see

a crystal amulet, a bird, perhaps a sparrow.
Surely, good luck. But maybe a crow. Or vulture?
Eyes widen to take in more wakefulness.

I watch the ghost, front and center
with the stretched-out t-shirt neck-sized gaping
mouth. There must be a dozen of them!

And it turns out that the rock is no rock at all.
Wonder how one's to sleep in such crowded space?
Eventually lids close against light and haunts.

A brief reprieve from reality until I wake
to the shaking of the house, the Giant's
shoes no longer in the clotheshorse.

Maybe Still Hope

Leaving this world you delivered a bird,
    dead, centered, broken,
        outside my window.

I lift her with a towel, fly her atop a hill,
    lay her behind a tree
        on the rabbit's grave.

I look to the sky and wish
    you both well. Crying
        until looking down on her closed eyes.

I imagine despite your fucking gruesome death,
    you tell me this: you are at peace.
        I pour wine into earth and turn away.

Leaves of Late November

Leaves spiral,
fall in three-fourths time,
dive a fast vertical twirl
as though knowing no end point,
float to and fro as in
downstream descent—all reach
the ground. They lie
on top of each other,
huddle against curbs, and
nestle in edging between
mulch and now-rust-colored lawns.
Leaves rest.
Shade in summer sun,
glory of early fall—they've
been through a lot.
I wish to take their place,
climb to the top of the most
naked tall tree and lay myself down.
Like on a bed of needles,
the spindly twigs might hold me
for their sheer numbers, and I
could blanket them and their branches
with my 98°. That's what I have of life—
heat and good intentions.

Kiss Planted

For My Dad, Ron E.
1940-2012

Tastes of salt, grey, tang of tobacco, sweet sweat like
ground mace, garlic and lemon paste have clung
to my lips for seven years. The last kiss planted
on your forehead, watered aplenty in your passing,
bloomed past grief, casting a shade of melancholy.

Makes it easy to window-stare for hours, meditate on
stones, gravity, creases, and spicy scents that endure.
I stop and double take whenever passing the smoke
of cigars or cherry pipe tobacco, increasingly rare.

I remember you, tall and linear in black and white in
the pipe days, before you lost teeth to hold the bit.
Less often in the cigar days, shorter,
built of 45 degree angles.

I don't begrudge that you forgot me. *Who
was the most me to you?* Parenting hosts
a fair amount of missing, the adorable
toddler, lost in a larger form.

Backing out of the room, I thanked you until my throat
was dry; you bedridden, slight beneath
the sheet. The same man I met at the door
when I was little with a kiss on the lips.

Inheritance

Bereft, but grateful he left
nothing to fight over. No
wealth, just children scattered
in different stages of struggle.
Years' worth of Happy Meal
toys and sealed bags of Easter
candy bought post-holiday.
Strollers, trikes, cars and trucks…
Nothing worth a damn in the study.
Then the garage, then the Scirocco.
Didn't run, but a son wanted
to fix it up, and a daughter
wanted to make it a planter.
A second-class relic must be
preserved. They thought and
fought. I took the cat. She pees all
over the house, but she's soft.

IV. In Motion

Underneath Quarantine

Because you could be anyone.
And I fall on a dime, let's bore
into quarantine, right through to the other
side, outside and inside "out" spaces.

Let's walk between shadows of ghosts of
crowds, shirking from the touch of points
of ponytails and jacket cuffs, down aisles,
between bookshelves, around dance-floors,

in gazebos above koi ponds. Because I don't
really know you. You could be everyone.
Let's share a kiss in memory of touch
and communion. Let's play Russian Roulette.

I feel lucky. Bet we fall in the uninfected 30 percent.
Because you have face and fingers and those
are remarkable things. It's already
been so long and some truths hurt. Because still

honesty. Let's quarantine together, spread
all the good and danger that radiates and
seeps. Let's meet. I'll buy the sake.
We can share a glass.

A Walk Together in Fall Rain

Her right-hand grips the handle of his umbrella;
 left—a warm cup of bitter caramel-colored coffee.
His left-hand cups her rib, arm cradled about her;
 right—grips a hot cup of black, sweet coffee.
She ducks thoughts of the first day of Fall, not enough
 yet stored for Winter.
He resists flight to a dry room, comforter, soft bed, aware
 clouds that fall on Maryland blow from Paris as well.
She thinks of things to hold onto—
 Summer tan, peace, his hair.
He thinks of things that give shelter—
 car roofs, faith, her eyes.
The rain syncopates against nylon,
 holds in echoes, breath, voices.

The One There Behind Me

I wear this pendant like a tag, the one
he gave me, wanting to be his. I think
of him and message, like missing
is mutual, like I always do, wearing
necklaces while loving the road its
melancholy and changing light. Plenty of
space in those betweens of
reflection with far away eyes when
scent or wind direction stir
up thoughts that drift to you.

In place at the right time too many
times for me to resist
anchoring in you. Nothing you'd welcome,
but you'd not deny me fantasies of
you keeping me awake across I-70,
I-10, down the lovely I-81 and dreadful
I-95 I loved for bringing me home to you.

Nowhere near where I'd head or return
now; uprooted, you displaced us both.
Seems my home lies in the way
you rub your chin in thought and exhale
your "yeah" when agreeing after
deliberation. I finger my gemstone, pull
thoughts back to him, wrestle
to lay down short-term memories.
Fancy him the love of my life with
some qualms because much
of the junket is past.
Through most of it I held to you.

A Few of My Favorite Lost Things

Hard to recall bits of beauty that scatter,
and hide from the wind made from the rush
to move on. Tough to even know bits of glitter
from light, although I'm not sure it matters.

Wrapped in missing I find too much gone in
folds that double and triple about my shoulders—
a prayer shawl, a shroud, a superhero cape.
My superpower is to smile

while I remember:
—the scent sweet of ginger-sweat and nicotine
soaked in a forehead I want lips upon, because
it's home and ought to have been enough.

—a name of staccato syllables rich in consonants that blend
sexy in print, all the lines and curves dancing side-by-side
—a wink from across a room—landscapes of profiles
—a rich voice that sounds of music, whether in speech or song.

Such things are to die or live for. Or to scatter back
on the breeze. Let them hide within slivers of tree bark,
under the shadows of dreams, behind the next man who smiles
for me, or let them evaporate to the clouds then rain down.

The County Fair

Outside the tilt-a-whirl, I seek thin
one o'clock shade left of a hat booth,
all audience and smiles. Waiting.
If he were here

we'd already have kissed
at least four times—under Genesis twice,
outside Alien Abduction, now. I'd
squint in the sun, after offering

him shade. I always like
the burn. Never minded the sting of
red, peeling, freckles deepened by sun,
even when teased by the mean kids.

My kid, eyes fixed on me, the compass rose,
jumps off the ride, runs back in line so fast
I'm dizzy. Squeeze my fingers hard
to ground myself. If he were here

we'd be holding hands. Weighed down by
a backpack with six liters of water, by-now-
smooshed PB&Js, and flannels unneeded
'till after dark, I'd still rise on tiptoes

to find his lips, while my boy spun too fast
to notice. And the fair would be as charming as
false nostalgia for the '50s, fitting
right in with our romance. We'd save voices

beneath shouting carnies, gas generators,
and music wailing, "Hold on, hold on to me."

Expectations High with the Simplest of Desires

Inspired by Diogenes the Cynic

Lamp in hand,
I search, even if in
rhetorical pursuit.
Take my sentimental
mug collection and
excess clothing in
a rainbow of sizes.
Leave my facile
cupped hands
and one warm
flannel. I'm also
happy to trade
armfuls of sweet,
ardent false promises
for the view of one
robust bough through
cracks in my clay walls.
I want less and
everything; roaming
the city on lookout
for one honest man.

Mutations in Thought

All the days in this long life
fill with such wonder of
words and sun dappled rivers,
indoor plumbing, cats, firelight,

fireflies, leaves shimmying on
limbs outstretched, and children
who care to tell the truth.
It's a wonder smiles ever fade.

But her head and his heart;
bedtime stories, tragic as
old witches shoved into ovens;
grief too fragile to put down

just yet—a world full of the
psychosomatically ill. Can't
will it otherwise. Minds see
what they see free of eyes.

So many forms of vision, like
the perception of the thought
planted deep within DNA,
"If only…"

The River

Steady before the drop that calls
for falling I fix my feet
as though braced in a fight
with a lover that's about to get
a little violent. Proximity to
precipice speaks of shattering
lines and edges, but for roots
that anchor earth to itself.
And the way she says, "Shhhh,"
not like the professional shushers at
children's theaters, but like the
old bunny in *Goodnight Moon*.
Dancing light and heady musk
inhaled into memory to be unfolded
later on my sick bed, with the hush
of the river's song. So I guess
I'm saying the falls are my
sister or my mother, if
family means solace.

They Don't Know the Bird Feeder Is Full

Blackie was a boss.
He'd'a jumped a top
the cylinder bird feeder
by now, swinging and
climbing; getting some
treats, alerting
other squirrels and
birds too. There'd be
a feast in that damp
yard today! But Blackie
ain't come around this
year. And as with other
things I didn't know
I'd miss—mixtapes,
all-nighters at Denny's,
Kevin's laugh—seems
seasons grow more and
more anticlimactic. Like
the New Year is just to
inhale a little less.
Still there's plenty of
movement out there
and these grey fellows.

Pecan Pie: A Great Reward

I hope there's pecan pie
in heaven. Or purgatory, maybe hell.
(It is awfully sweet.) Wherever you are.
Maybe reincarnated, a rising

third grader. Are you scared to return
to school or do you just want to see friends?
I pray the boy you are, that doesn't remember
me, won't get Covid; won't lose sense

of taste, and that your Mama who I hope
is a little like me bakes you pecan pie. I buy
pecans a couple of times a year. A few times
the cupboards go bare and we eat the nuts raw.

I regret not making pie in your honor yet.
And feel disloyal loving peas too. I sprinkle
them over salad, spaghetti, curry; I remember
your revulsion, gags, scrunched face. Sorry.

But I order samosas every chance I get and made
Dairy Queen a tradition with my boy, until Blizzards
made him sick. Funny to anchor memories of you
in food, although irony reminds me of you most.

You with your hard-earned anorexia. Still couldn't lift
you when legs gave out. Beaches remind
me of you, weightlessness of water, how you never learned
to swim, how the ocean scares and renews.

Eyes of the Dead

Flying past hoping the fare is enough,
although it never was this side of breath,

he sees, or rather perceives through coins
and deflated eyes, the last cricket of the season

chirping in twilight relief. Often nights
can't be endured, exhausting to wrangle

with the sun in squints and shadows; some
nights wrap so gently in darkness.

Better he turns to fire and burn
than fight what rises every day.

Wind

Wind out of control, loose hair waves
jackets and skirts fly from legs

and chests, trailers cross solid
yellow lines. No matter how still

you hold the wheel, or struggle to adjust,
the truck sways for gusts. Hold

my affect to over-correct for your squalls—
north, south, east, west, sad tales, wishes,

fights to escape and stay still. Often I ask
the weatherman, but he gets it wrong.

Your hints scatter away. So few
make it and you don't want me to know.

This love of what grows wild flowers and tickles
my skin is erratic, uncertain, hard to stare down.

Epilogue

She forgot the last kiss shared, but finally
    understood marriage:
        to share another's lips in perpetuity.

She couldn't plant them in time,
        but recalled
a string of pre-kisses in cars, dance halls, beds, under stars,
suspension of mouths meeting,
        inhaling each other's breath,
until skin grazed skin.
        Each was her little grasp on immortality.

Separated, divorced, single, dating—words that sound like
potential,
        like string lights, like the opening bars of "Drift Away,"
            but feel the opposite when reaching into
            the lampshade to turn the lights out.

About the Author

Kristin Kowalski Ferragut teaches, plays guitar, hikes, supports her children in becoming who they are meant to be, and enjoys the vibrant writing community in the DMV. She is the author of the children's book *Becoming the Enchantress: A Magical Transgender Tale* (Loving Healing Press, 2021). Her poetry has appeared in *Beltway Quarterly, Bourgeon, Mojave He[Art] Review, Anti-Heroin Chic, Fledgling Rag, and Little Patuxent Review* among others. For more information visit her website www.kristinskiferragut.com.